# DOGS TO THE RESCUE!

# THERAPY DOGS

By Sara Green

BELLWETHER MEDIA • MINNEAPOLIS, MN

Jump into the cockpit and take flight with Pilot books. Your journey will take you on high-energy adventures as you learn about all that is wild, weird, fascinating, and fun!

This edition first published in 2014 by Bellwether Media, Inc.

No part of this publication may be reproduced in whole or in part without written permission of the publisher. For information regarding permission, write to Bellwether Media, Inc., Attention: Permissions Department, 5357 Penn Avenue South, Minneapolis, MN 55419.

Library of Congress Cataloging-in-Publication Data

Green, Sara, 1964-
Therapy dogs / by Sara Green.
    pages cm. – (Pilot: Dogs to the rescue!)
Includes bibliographical references and index.
Summary: "Engaging images accompany information about therapy dogs. The combination of high-interest subject matter and narrative text is intended for students in grades 3 through 7"–Provided by publisher.
ISBN 978-1-60014-960-3 (hardcover : alk. paper)
1. Dogs–Therapeutic use–Juvenile literature. I. Title.
RM931.D63G74 2014
615.8'5158–dc23

                                    2013012177

Printed in the United States of America, North Mankato, MN.

# TABLE OF CONTENTS

# CHARLIE THE THERAPY DOG

Nursing home residents gather in the **common area**. Many are in wheelchairs. They are eager to meet a special visitor. Soon, a small sheepdog named Charlie arrives with his **handler**. Charlie spends time with each person. He enjoys sitting with them while they pet him. He also likes to perform a few tricks. He shakes hands, twirls, and waves. The residents take turns throwing a ball for Charlie to fetch.

Later, Charlie and his handler visit people who are too ill to leave their beds. Each person spends a few minutes petting Charlie. Some ask to snuggle with him in their bed. All too soon, it is time for Charlie and his handler to leave. But he will return again. Charlie loves bringing joy to the nursing home residents!

# WHAT IS A THERAPY DOG?

Therapy dogs and their handlers visit people in nursing homes, hospitals, schools, and other places. These dogs bring comfort and friendship to the people they visit. Many people feel happy and relaxed while petting dogs. Often, they find it easier to connect with a dog than with other people. This is because dogs are fun to talk to! Some children would rather read aloud to therapy dogs than to people. The dogs help them develop their reading skills and confidence.

Therapy dogs sit quietly while people pet them, hug them, or read to them. Large dogs usually sit next to people, while small dogs often sit on their laps. Many dogs also perform simple tricks during their visits. Therapy dogs bring cheer to everyone they meet!

CLASS
PRESIDENT
by Johanna Hurwitz

Many therapy dogs do more than visit people. They also assist professional staff when they **treat** patients. The dogs **motivate** patients in many ways. Patients talk to the dogs to practice speech skills. The dogs also encourage patients with **mobility** challenges to practice moving. These patients walk to the dogs, throw balls to them, or use them to help with balance.

Therapy dogs sometimes help people with memory loss. Some people forget the faces or names of friends and relatives. They may not remember important events in their lives. However, the dogs often remind them of their own pets. Seeing the dogs brings them happiness. Therapy dogs help people with mental health conditions, too. Their presence often boosts people's spirits and increases their self-confidence.

# A GENTLE TEMPERAMENT

Therapy dogs come in all breeds and sizes. What matters most is a dog's **temperament**. Therapy dogs are friendly, patient, and gentle. They receive pets and hugs without barking, nipping, or jumping on people. Therapy dogs are **obedient** and follow their handlers' directions. Sometimes, older dogs make better therapy dogs than puppies. This is because dogs usually become calmer with age.

Therapy dogs must be comfortable around wheelchairs, **walkers**, and other unusual equipment. They must be able to **tolerate** loud noises, crowds, and new smells. Some therapy dogs must be at ease riding in elevators. All must be patient with **grooming**. Handlers bathe and brush their dogs before beginning their visits.

# Breeds of Therapy Dogs

**Golden Retriever**

**Leonberger**

**Shetland Sheepdog**

**Labrador Retriever**

# Profile: Golden Retriever

## Intelligence
The Golden Retriever is the fourth smartest dog breed. The dog will obey new commands almost immediately.

## Size
Height: 20 to 24 inches (51 to 61 centimeters)

Weight: 50 to 80 pounds (23 to 36 kilograms)

## Characteristics
A Golden Retriever is loyal and eager to please. The dog is friendly and can make its partner and strangers feel comfortable.

# A TEAM EFFORT

Therapy dogs usually belong to their handlers. They **volunteer** as a team to visit and help others. The handlers must be outgoing, friendly, and social. They need to have a positive attitude and enjoy making conversation with strangers. Handlers must be sensitive to the needs of everyone they visit. For example, some people may be too ill to chat. They may prefer to pet the dogs in silence. Others may welcome conversation. Handlers always check with staff members before they begin their visits. This helps them plan their visits to fit people's special needs.

Although the handlers care about the people they visit, the dogs are their top concern. Handlers are always aware of the health and safety of their dogs. If a dog appears anxious or ill, the handler will cut a visit short. Good handlers always give their dogs breaks when necessary.

# TRAINED TO HEAL

Therapy dog training often begins when the dogs are puppies. Handlers teach them basic **obedience skills**. The dogs learn to walk on a leash at the handler's side, even through crowds. They also learn to ignore food and other distractions.

When the dogs are ready, their handlers bring them to public places. There, the dogs learn to stay calm in crowds. Handlers invite people to pet their dogs. This way, the dogs learn to accept attention from strangers.

Most dogs train for at least one year. Then they are ready to take a **certification** test. To pass the test, the dogs must have a variety of skills. They must follow commands and behave well in public. They must be comfortable around crutches, loud noises, and other dogs. The test often includes ear tugs, tail pulls, and tight hugs. Dogs that react calmly are on their way to becoming great therapy dogs!

# Different from Service Dogs

Therapy dogs and service dogs are different. Unlike therapy dogs, service dogs are not considered pets. These highly trained dogs perform a wide range of tasks for only one person. They are also allowed by law to accompany their partners anywhere.

Once they are certified, therapy dogs can visit people in places where other dogs are usually not allowed. They often wear a special vest or bandana to show that they are therapy dogs.

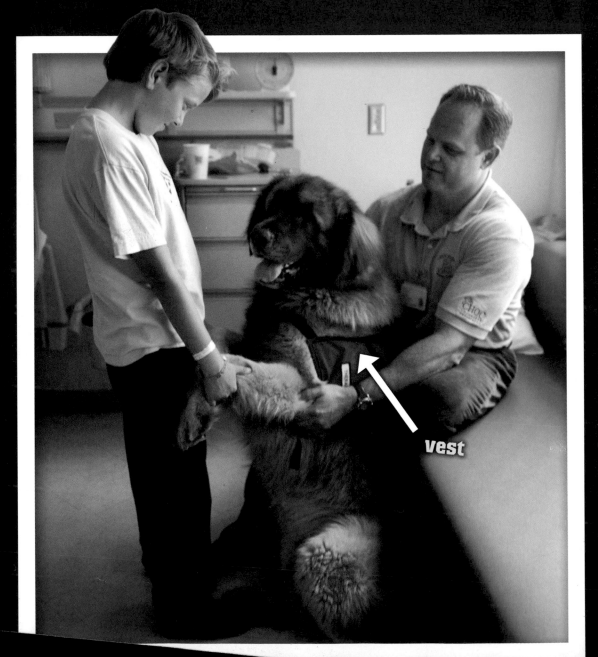

vest

## Resident Therapy Dogs

Some therapy dogs live with the people they serve. Many nursing homes and hospitals have their own resident therapy dogs. Every day, these beloved canine companions bring people great joy.

Each therapy dog provides friendship and comfort to many people. The handler finds out who would like a visit from a therapy dog. Then the team moves from person to person. Sometimes they spend only a few minutes with a person. Other times the visit lasts longer. During the visits, many people enjoy talking about their own dogs. They share happy memories and funny stories.

Therapy dogs usually perform their work for a few hours per week. When work is finished, a therapy dog returns to being a pet. Now it is free to behave just like a regular dog.

# HAVING WHAT IT TAKES

Many people enjoy volunteering to help others. They like the idea of bringing their pet dog along as a therapy dog. But how do they know if their dog would make a good therapy dog? After all, being a therapy dog is not always easy. Dogs must show affection to strangers. They must be patient and gentle when strangers hug and pet them.

Owners interested in therapy dog training can give their dogs an easy test. They can take their dogs to noisy, crowded locations. Here, owners can observe their dogs' behavior. The dogs should be friendly and outgoing with strangers. They must remain relaxed and follow commands with ease. A dog with these qualities might have what it takes to be a therapy dog!

# SMOKY: THE FIRST THERAPY DOG

A Yorkshire Terrier named Smoky was the first therapy dog. Smoky weighed only 4 pounds (1.8 kilograms). She belonged to a World War II soldier named Bill Wynne. In 1944, Bill became sick and had to spend time in a hospital. Smoky was allowed to visit him. Soon, the other patients wanted visits from Smoky, too. Many of them were wounded soldiers.

The nurses in the hospital noticed the positive effect that Smoky had. Patients felt better and seemed happier when the little dog was around. Charles Mayo, a doctor at the hospital, began to bring Smoky with him whenever he visited patients. At night, Dr. Mayo allowed Smoky to sleep in Bill's bed. Smoky spent the next 12 years working as a therapy dog. This tiny canine brought smiles to many people!

Smoky

**Yorkshire Terrier**

**A Popular Breed**
Smoky's popularity sparked people's interest in Yorkshire Terriers, Today they are one of the most popular dog breeds!

# GLOSSARY

**certification**—official recognition that a dog has mastered specific job skills

**common area**—an area that all residents of a place can use

**grooming**—cleaning a dog's coat

**handler**—a person who is responsible for a highly trained dog

**mobility**—the ability to move the body with ease

**motivate**—to make someone want to do something

**obedience skills**—skills such as sit, stay, down, and come

**obedient**—follows commands

**temperament**—personality or nature

**tolerate**—to allow without complaint

**treat**—to give medical aid

**volunteer**—to do something for others without expecting money in return

**walkers**—devices that support people when they walk

# TO LEARN MORE

## AT THE LIBRARY

Bozzo, Linda. *Therapy Dog Heroes*. Berkeley Heights, N.J.: Bailey Books/Enslow Publishers, 2011.

Hutmacher, Kimberly. *Therapy Dogs*. Mankato, Minn.: Capstone Press, 2011.

Tagliaferro, Linda. *Therapy Dogs*. New York, N.Y.: Bearport Pub. Co., 2005.

## ON THE WEB

Learning more about therapy dogs is as easy as 1, 2, 3.

1. Go to www.factsurfer.com.

2. Enter "therapy dogs" into the search box.

3. Click the "Surf" button and you will see a list of related Web sites.

With factsurfer.com, finding more information is just a click away.

# INDEX